9/23

POLAR
BEARS

by Jacqueline S. Cotton

D1025630

Lerner Publications Company • Minneapolis

FR: Level G
Bib # 533522

To my son, Zachary

This book is available in two editions:
Library binding by Lerner Publications Company, a division of Lerner Publishing Group
Soft cover by First Avenue Editions, an imprint of Lerner Publishing Group
241 First Avenue North
Minneapolis, MN 55401 U.S.A.

Website address: www.lernerbooks.com

Library of Congress Cataloging-in-Publication Data

Cotton, Jacqueline S.
    Polar bears / by Jacqueline S. Cotton.
        p.   cm. — (Pull ahead books)
    Summary: A simple introduction to polar bears,
describing their physical characteristics, natural
habitat, hunting skills, eating habits, and care of cubs.
        ISBN: 0–8225–3776–1 (lib. bdg. : alk. paper)
        ISBN: 0–8225–9890–6 (pbk. : alk. paper)
        1. Polar bear—Juvenile literature. [1. Polar bear.
    2. Bears.] I. Title. II. Series.
    QL737.C27C675 2004
    599.786—dc22   2003016547

Manufactured in the United States of America
1 2 3 4 5 6 — JR — 09 08 07 06 05 04

What is this furry, white animal?

This is a polar bear.

Polar bears live in a cold place called the *Arctic*. They live on the snowy shore along icy water.

Polar bears have thick, white fur.
Their fur keeps them warm.

How do you keep warm?

Thick fur on the bottom of their feet keeps polar bears from slipping on the snow and ice.

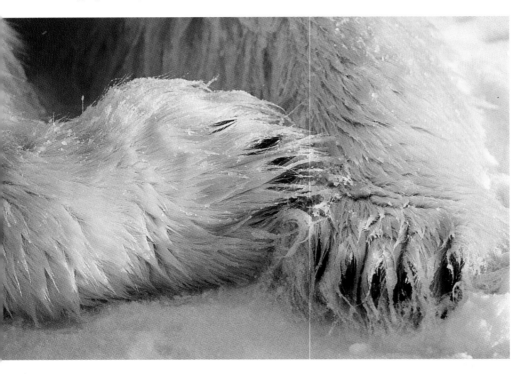

Sharp claws help them grip the ice.

Polar bears are good swimmers.

Their front feet make powerful paddles. They use their back feet to steer.

Polar bears can swim a long way
without stopping to rest.

They can swim underwater for as
much as two minutes.

A polar bear gets out of the water.
It shakes the water off its fur.

What other animals do this?

A polar bear's white fur is the same color as the ice and snow. It is called *camouflage*.

Camouflage helps a polar bear to hunt. It is hard for other animals to see a polar bear in the snow.

Polar bears are *predators.*
Predators hunt and eat other animals.

Polar bears hunt mainly seals.

This polar bear is looking into a seal's *breathing hole*.

A seal comes up for air. And the polar bear will grab it.

Sometimes polar bears just wait
for seals to show up.

A polar bear will wait a long time
to catch a seal.

A polar bear
hunts in its
home range.

A home range is where
a polar bear lives.

Polar bears usually hunt and live alone.

But sometimes they come together to hunt.

Polar bears take naps after they hunt.

They sleep on the ice and snow.

Where do you sleep?

In winter some female polar bears sleep in a *den*. A den is a safe, cozy place dug in the snow.

The female polar bear
has babies in the den.

Baby polar bears are called *cubs.*

A female polar bear usually
has two cubs.

What helps polar bear cubs grow?

Polar bear cubs drink their mother's milk.

The milk helps the cubs grow quickly.

In the spring, the mother polar bear and her cubs leave the den. Polar bears slide down the hills for fun.

What do you do for fun?

It is naptime. Polar bear cubs
snuggle up to their mother to
keep warm.

The mother polar bear takes good care of her cubs. She teaches them how to hunt.

One day these cubs will be big
enough to hunt and live alone.

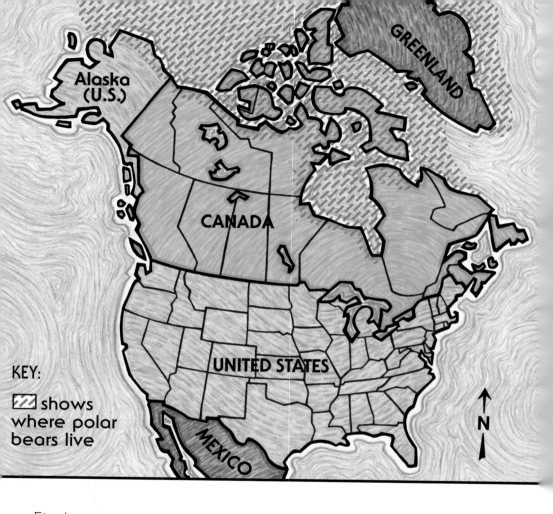

KEY:

 shows
where polar
bears live

Alaska
(U.S.)

GREENLAND

CANADA

UNITED STATES

MEXICO

N

Find your state or province on this map.
Do polar bears live near you?